PAINFULLY LIGHTWORKERS JOURNEY

BY
ERICA L. SPENCER

Copyright © 2023 Erica L. Spencer.

All rights reserved. No part of this publication may be reproduced, distributed, or transmitted in any form or by any means, including photocopying, recording, or other electronic or mechanical methods, without the prior written permission of the publisher, except in the case of brief quotations embodied in critical reviews and certain other noncommercial uses permitted by copyright law.

ISBN:

CONTENTS

Dedication	*3*
Preface	*4*
Chapter 1 Childhood Memories	*6*
Chapter 2 The Misunderstood Empathic Child	*18*
Chapter 3 Seeing And Feeling Life Energetically	*32*
Chapter 4 Seeking Acceptance	*41*
Chapter 5 Confusion	*47*
Chapter 6 Education	*54*
Chapter 7 Practice	*61*
Chapter 8 The Evolution Of The Healer In Light Work	*68*
Chapter 9 Spiritual Awakening	*74*
Chapter 10 The Dark Night Of The Soul	*86*
Chapter 11 The Quantum Field	*92*
Chapter 12 Conclusion	*98*

DEDICATION

This book is dedicated to the inner child within everyone who has had to or still needs to recover and heal from their childhood.

PREFACE

This is my story, it is not a detailed version of it, just an overview to describe the types of programs and projections that I had to endure in order to figure out how to understand them better. This is not an attempt to place blame on anyone for the cycles of suffering we have all endured and participated in as we are living in a blameless generation at this time. The reason for writing this book was to give a description of what I endured through the eyes of a developing empathic child who was born into a family that was not able to cope with their emotions and instead found maladaptive ways of responding to their stress and expressing themselves to each-other. This is the case for many children born into poverty or to parents who are not developmentally ready to guide or care for them in a way that would be nurturing to their unique gifts and attributes.

As someone who has been able to see beyond the psychological enslavement that adults tend to find themselves in, I still suffered immensely working my way through to self-liberation. Discovering a healing process to help others who have found themselves lost and locked in their own minds without access to their own hearts has been my lifelong journey. Not just because I needed to liberate myself from it but also because I want to share this knowledge with others so that anyone who resonates with my story can benefit and be inspired from the information that I have discovered pertaining on how to treat and heal it. I hope that this book activates and inspires the inner child within you to connect back again so that you may also discover what it has observed and recorded for you to help you on your way. Domestic violence, sexual abuse, manipulation, bullying, envy, betrayal, abandonment, judgement, an over sexualized culture, patriarchal behaviors, extreme need for control, misogyny, deception, wrath, lust, and greed are just a few of the main dark truths that I've had to witness and experience through others in my life's journey so far. These dark truths are embedded deeply into many of the systems the we as humans rely on to navigate and live out our existence in. These systems have turned corrupt and it is important that we face this head on and deal with it appropriately not just for ourselves and our own healing process but for our children and for future generations to come. I write this story to speak up as a voice for the inner child of all who are still trying to recover from their childhood. My hopes are that many others will also want to share their stories and observations in return to help create better programs and systems to be put in place to support a healthier, less hurtful and more peaceful and loving way of moving through this human experience together.

CHAPTER 1
CHILDHOOD MEMORIES

It wasn't just another night in my life, but an experience. The moment I left the sacred place that I had not told anyone about, it hit me; The top of my head tingled, and my body presented with goosebumps. It coerced me to ruminate as a sullen reality stretched before my raddled eyes, and I could discern the beauty that lingered around me. It emerged from people I passed, and somehow, I could see it. Their Light. The feel of their energetic frequency pierced through my soul just as the night wind flew in my hair. I was overstimulated by the clutter of information that I was receiving, and it was overwhelming, the network of the emotions in my mind. Each piece of information that came through showed me the past, the present, and the future all at once, not in a visual way but as an emotional download holding all types of messages to serve as a catalyst to activate more pathways in the human brain. These messages were filled with ways to help them connect back to their light so that they may liberate themselves of the emotional pain & confusion they were presently trapped in. As a child, I didn't really understand what to do with all of this information.

The bike ride back home, however, took me longer than usual. As I allowed myself to observe all of the information that I had received for the day, I also wondered if I would make it home in time to watch my favorite television show. I enjoyed nature in its rawest form, it soothed me and it centered me in a way nothing else could – I would always prefer nature over anything else, even the television shows that I watched. Growing up in an extremely seasonal environment in Upstate NY I would cherish the longer days where the sun blanketed everything with its light and its warmth. Everything I would gaze at in nature sent me into a state of pensiveness. The information I would receive would inspire me forever and prevent me from diving back into the world of pseudo smiles.

Back home, the energy was very different from what I experienced in nature or even while passing others while I rode my bike. The desolation inside of my home altered me as I walked back in from being out, and an eccentric placidity took over; I felt miserable about everything but not defeated. I had a lot of fight left in me. Forsaken in contemplation, I looked down at my clothes. I slowly became aware of my physical environment, especially the walls that had watched me grow into a girl and knew all of my secrets, but enclosed me away from the natural world that helped me feel so balanced. They appeared sad for some reason; maybe they were reflecting my brooding heart – a heart that would ache with every beat but not hurt. Instead, it would allow me to see beyond; the walls in my room, white and gloomy.

Suddenly, an intricate feeling hit me as I got distracted, musingly watching the walls; I had never craved affection like that before. It bothered me. This was not the first time I craved affection; I was not foreign to this feeling, yet there was something about it I could not grasp. Prudently, I returned to the world I like to refer to as the world of confusion and pain when I heard my mother's voice again after our small argument that sent me wandering in the woods.

I felt an abrupt rush of thoughts in my mind. They circled and made me think about nature. From a very young age, I had a peculiar propensity towards nature. I don't know how I developed it, but others found it rather idiosyncratic – the amount of time I spent with plants rather than people. It is probably because of that one time a tree saved my life, the first time I witnessed nature in its most loving & purest form. But I guess I am mixing events and getting too ahead of myself, so let's start from the beginning.

When I indulged in the retrospection even deeper, another memory that rang in my ears was a sound – a concealed cry. My mother was on the hospital bed, and her cries were piercing like a morose agony in the ears of all the attendants and nurses. From there, the next thing I could recall was my grandfather yelling at my mom and blaming me for ruining her life. I stood by my mother's side, looking down at the floor, trying to understand his anger towards us. I felt his pain, and it was not all pain from anything my mother did; it was plain that he had not processed from a previous marriage where he had lost his first wife to death and then all of his children to her family. My grandfather lived with so much guilt, shame, and grief that instead of finding a way to heal and process it, he indulged in escapism through alcohol and projected it out onto his family.

But when I grew up and took on a new form of evolution, I understood more deeply why he felt it necessary to project his pain onto us. even though it wasn't right, he didn't know any better at the time.

When my mother had me, she was still a teenager. My grandfather was disappointed in her and he believed that I came between her and her ability to have a successful future. I feel as if my grandfather had high hopes for my mother to cover up his pain, he felt for leaving his other children behind and to justify his lack of efforts to fight for them to stay in his life. My mother, indeed, was a phenomenal woman. She was remarkable, though her choices pushed her to a reality she couldn't fully control. Although she never admitted it, the life she was destined to live bothered her; I could see it but couldn't express it using the right words.

However, there were instances when I would stand up for myself and try to help her realize things that I was picking up on from her energy field. But since I was just a child, my mother never really considered, or should I say, understood me; she would get mad and say things like, "Where did you learn to say that?" or "From where is that coming from?"

You see, I have always been an observer since I was a child and possessed the ability to see beyond people; hence, I was often confused. Where everyone saw the person on the outside, I also saw everyone for who they were on the inside, and I accepted all parts. both the light and the dark. I guess this was the reason why I was very talkative whenever necessary – something people despised about me. I felt like I had a deep connection with them because I could connect to their soul, through unity consciousness. Although I never realized why back then, when I think about it now, I understand – most others I've come across seem to prefer staying in an illusion & in a silenced reality that they have built around themselves, to keep themselves safe, which helps them to feel adequate and content. And whenever you cast a picture of what's real or possibly real outside of their beliefs, they tend to take offense and get defensive; the same was the case with my mother.

Often, she dismissed me, and lock herself in her bathroom and cry. The routine was that she would cry inside the bathroom while I would sob outside of it. I would cry with her as I could feel the pain that she carried from how she had been treated as a teenage single mother while she grew me in her belly and after she had me, and I could feel her pain from the abandonment and abuse that she had endured from the men who she had chosen to share her heart with. I could feel her resentment toward me as I had been a catalyst to making her reality more difficult. I was a burden to her, and she would sometimes remind me of it when faced with a conflict between us. I didn't just cry just for her either; I also cried for myself, knowing that my mother would never be able to love me as deeply as I wish she could because of all this.

My mother was beautiful so she didn't have a hard time attracting men. So, I can imagine it was hard for her to discern, especially after she became pregnant and was faced with harsh criticism from everyone around her. First, there was my father, who abandoned her, but also abandoned me. He was in prison for the first three years of my life, and I didn't meet him until I was six years old. I guess I was so used to his absence in my life that when we met, I felt a disconnect from him and our father daughter relationship was never consistent. There were no authentic or affectionate emotions. But I could see the light in him, I admired his light and I resonated with parts of it, but he would never allow a real connection to stay consistent with me as his partners would always interfere with his visitation and relationship with me. This never made sense to me other than what I could sense, which was always some form of jealousy and mistrust towards my mother from them. This still confused me as a child, why I was the one who was punished for it. Thus, I never really had a chance to have a real and true connection with my biological father without interference.

It felt like I had a third eye to see the good in others. I mostly focused on that as all of the other stuff I could feel, when triggered, seemed to want to cause more chaos for me, so I continued to live this way until my immediate parents would eventually become abusive to me by projecting their pain onto me. As a child I just wanted to hug them when they started to emotionally react hoping to bring them back to a happy place but I wasn't sure how to do this as they all had different reactions to me and sometimes those reactions were filled with more rage.

When it comes to other men my mother invited into her life, they seemed wounded and they were always abusive in some way. I was exposed to a lot of domestic violence as a child. I would often ponder why my mother kept up with men treating her the way that they did. What made things even worse was that their abuse was not only limited to my mother. They would physically and emotionally abuse me too. One even sexually abused me and threatened to cause malicious harm to me and my mother if I had told anyone. They all had an anger inside them that they didn't know how to process and they just kept continuously projecting it onto us just like my grandfather did. Only they didn't use alcohol to escape from themselves, they used fear and control and manipulation to keep us under their rule. To help themselves feel better about the stuff that they refused to deal with and face within themselves. But they didn't understand that by doing this, they only continued to feed the worst parts of themselves and they continued to release these cycles of suffering onto us and anyone else who would come close to us.

So far, you can tell how much of a painful and lonely childhood I endured. Even my cousins disliked me because I seemed overly sensitive and younger; the girls who were older thought I was weird and damaged of course this perception was probably fed to them by their parents, and maybe I even gave off a distress signal in my energy field, though the boys who were younger than me, they seemed to accept me. But since I was a girl, we had nothing in common. from what I was led to believe anyway. As for the kids in the neighborhood, even they thought I was weird and would hesitate to play with me. What made their behavior even weirder towards me was that they would sometimes play with me if they were alone. But in a group, they would make fun of me for being a bit different.

In my life, where most people seemed to be annoyed by me and judged me as a child that probably shouldn't have been born, one person who I felt truly understood me was my grandmother. I think she was the reason why I grew up loving nature. My grandmother had around ten to twenty plants on her window. I would watch her water them whenever I was at her house; it intrigued me. Youngspirited, I gradually helped her and began watering plants on my own. It filled my delight. This was when I realized that I wasn't actually alone because this may sound a little weird, but I felt the energy of the plants, which was when I noticed that they seemed to be more balanced and loving than the energy of other human beings around me. So, when that tree saved my life, everything changed.

One day, I was at my aunt's house. My cousins and I were in a large tree. We spent a lot of time in trees as children as they had a treehouse in their backyard and we were always trying to make every tree a new place to hang out in. I can't tell you what type of tree it was but the energy of it felt like home. when my aunt's bellow called my cousin inside the house for dinner. I hadn't been invited to eat with them that night, so I decided to stay back and spend more time with the tree while they went in to eat. While I lay there on one of the branches, I had this great idea of climbing to the top of the tree to look out over the rooftops of the neighboring houses. lost in my thoughts and excitement to reach the top of the tree, my foot slipped, and I started to fall. At that moment, everything came to an abrupt halt. I could no longer make out my surroundings, except that I was falling and going to either break some bones or die. But before I hit the ground, my hand suddenly caught the lowest tree branch not in a gripping way but in an energetic velcro way, and the tree held me in the air from the branch as I dangled from it with one arm. I quickly latched onto the branch with my other hand and pulled myself up to lay fully across it and I hugged it tightly while also thanking it for keeping me safe from harm. It felt like the tree, in all of its soft and nurturing power, had saved my life. Everything happened so fast, none of it made logical sense to me, it was an experience nobody would understand or believe in the way that I had perceived it. This left me feeling a bit disconnected from others which is why I became even closer to nature as a result.

My mother's voice carried sullen energy when she would call out to me as it echoed in my room. I was a bit mad at her throughout my childhood, but when I became a teenager, I had also become more cognizant of my surroundings. I developed a better sense of comprehension, especially of emotions. I understood that her grief came from a very special place, which made her believe that the abusive love she had welcomed into her life was what she felt she deserved and was what she was familiar with, even if it affected me. But I, as her daughter, knew she was not doing this on purpose. She was someone who had a difficult time expressing herself. She was trapped in her own pain, blocked from her heart's ability to receive the love she truly deserved. Anytime I would trigger this knowing within her she would lash out on me and refuse to hear anything I was noticing or seeing in her energy field. Maybe I was doing it wrong, I probably was, but at least I was trying to figure out how to break through these limitations that she somehow became bound in. At least I knew we all deserved to live and feel better than what we were tolerating as individuals and as a unit. I knew in my heart I couldn't let this continue to circulate throughout our existence. It was holding us back from who we were meant to grow into and become. I could see her light, her potential, her gifts but she didn't even have access to them as she was blocked from all of it, because of the pain, from the abuse, from the restrictions that she believed she had been chained in. And she continued to perpetuate these limitations until it started to affect her body and break down her organs to where she started to become physically ill from the pain and the suffering that she was carrying. This is partially why I decided to educate myself about psychology and emotion as an adult, so I could make sense of this painful existence that I was observing and growing up in.

With time, I started to understand how to deal with everything that I was carrying from what was projected onto me and from what I was taught and programmed with along the way from my abusers and from others around me. Which meant that I had to silence myself and partially conform to their rules and regulations as a child and a young adult, in order to survive through the madness that I did not want to identify with because most of it wasn't even mine to work through but because they couldn't see what I could see, I had to keep record until I could express my findings as an adult when I would become secure enough in my own being to speak my truth confidently and with love, so that I wouldn't further cause harm to the cycles of suffering that so many already endure and have no idea how to process or clear themselves of.

CHAPTER 2
THE MISUNDERSTOOD EMPATHIC CHILD

Growing up, I was always referred to as a 'black sheep' of the family. It was not because I was disrespectful or had developed bad habits; it was just that I presented differently. I just came into a family with a strong passion for life and with what I believe a higher consciousness than them. Looking back, I remember them often being annoyed with me for always trying to strive to find beauty in everything or motivation to strive higher. I ran at a faster pace with a shorter attention span than most and this also frustrated them. It was obvious to me after some time that not everybody was actively trying to do their best to figure life out. As I recall, they were just really defensive around me, as if I was disrupting their energy fields. I felt like everybody around me was either trying to compete with me, avoid me altogether or trying to dim me. In other words, there was a type of resistance in my family towards me and it was all the result of how differently I behaved & perceived the world from them. Instead of being curious about my unique perspective and wonder I was rejected and shunned and talked poorly of due to not being able to conform to the rules or always behave in the ways that were expected of me. I often found myself face to face with the demons of jealousy, envy, control and lust in my environments, which was simply suffocating and, at times, reached high levels of absurdity.

For example, when I got my menstrual cycle for the first time, my mother made sure to let me know that my older cousin had cried because I got it before her. She was angry about it, she believed that it marked your way into being a woman and that she should have been the one to get it before me because she was a year older. I didn't really understand why my menstrual cycle upset others emotionally when it was about me and not them, but for some reason she made it about her and took that away from me. We were also always comparing each other's weights, seeing who had the lowest weight and thinnest waist. At the time, I didn't really understand why my cousins behaved this way; part of me just wanted to be comfortable in my own skin and not have to conform or adhere to another person's expectations. But this became a ritual every time we saw each other. We weighed ourselves in front of each other and told each other where we rated in the world. You can imagine where I would mostly end up in this competition. I only participated in this because it was some level of acceptance that I was able to experience, even if I wasn't seen as the best or as the shining star. As an outcast, you have to conform to some degree. I had such a strong spirit about me that it was hard for me to do this even when I wanted to feel like I fit in. I wanted to expand and stretch myself out in all experiences to feel them fully and experience them fully; how everyone was operating around me didn't feel right. I Always stayed very observant of my surroundings, I questioned a lot of things that just felt unjust to me. And, often, I would sometimes feel overstimulated from not knowing how to process all of the information that I was receiving and reflecting on, & also feeling powerless to change any given situation that singled me out as some sort of problem or issue.

Growing up with my family I just felt like everyone was constantly either trying to point fingers at me for any wrong or out of the ordinary that happened or find any excuse to punish me. Me being the odd one out was always a point of gossip; I would hear my mother talking poorly of me on the phone to her sisters; they always made it like I was a form of entertainment to gossip about as some sort of weird negative force.

I guess I just got under the skin because I was triggering them as, being an empath, my frequency would just pull internal wounds to the surface, making whoever was spending the most time with me become aware of what was going on inside of them so that they can clear it. I would even sometimes ask them or bring stuff up to them so they would understand why they were becoming irritable, but it would just anger them. I knew in my heart somehow that I was directly letting them know what I was picking up on. They would deny it and not validate any of my claims, thus teaching me to not trust myself as I grew older. This was extremely frustrating. Holding and feeling into so much heavy information that nobody wanted to face or take accountability for.

My frequency is designed to inspire and motivate others and to help inspire them to shift their frequencies back into natural alignment. But I guess, in a household blocked from their true nature, it did the reverse and triggered them to the point where they would get defensive around me and wanted to either be hostile against me or send me away from them so they didn't have to feel or experience what I was bringing up within them. For the longest time I was able to see what was really going on and that it wasn't me it was their stuff but too many others over time started to weigh on me and make me question my own self-worth and truth. I spent a lot of time alone as a child which looking back now, I'm not upset about, because I am easily able to recover information that I was processing and storing the entire time. That was how a lot of my childhood experiences went with other relatives and close friends.

Thinking more about it, I believe part of the reason why my family put such emphasis on conforming was because of the fact that most of my extended family were very religious. They were of the Pentecostal denomination. I felt as if the faith was very restrictive and had unnecessary rules. I didn't fully fit in with my cousins because they followed the faith more closely than I could. My mother didn't even try to attend church at all; she never had an interest in following any type of faith. So naturally I adopted it as much as I could as I did wish to connect with God and I did feel more of a connection to myself in a loving way when I would attend services. I was prohibited from being in the choir and I was singled out by the pastor and the congregation for certain events since I wasn't following all of the rules closely. I accepted my fate with this because at that point, this was how all of my life was going and I was used to not having full privileges anywhere.

It was all kind of sad, really. I felt like I could help because I was observing things that others either weren't acknowledging or didn't want to acknowledge. However, whenever I would bring up the issue, they would just silence me or make an argument about them being older and hence wiser than me. Therefore, invalidating my insights and views of what I was perceiving and picking up on.

Relating to this, the relationship between Mom and I was especially tense at times. She complained about me to all of her sisters because, to her, I was even more challenging than normal because I just couldn't understand why she was parenting me the way she was, and I would always point it out; I didn't feel like it was very loving or nurturing. I observed that she did the basics when it came to being a parent & showing me how to manage my emotions. She was able to provide the basic stuff, such as shelter, clothes, and food which she would always make a point to me when we argued. As if I was ungrateful. She didn't understand that I was begging for guidance on subjects she had not mastered yet and that I was asking her to help me figure it out by wanting to figure hers out. She was not motivated to heal or process her pain, she was just motivated to stay strong and survive thus, leaving me to my own demise on how to understand myself enough as a young highly sensitive/ empathic child to figure out how to self-regulate or self soothe while feeling overstimulated. I picked up some maladaptive coping mechanisms in childhood as a result of living in an environment that didn't seem to understand any of the things I was experiencing.

I got along even less with my father figures – my mother would marry twice. She was single for a short time in which we were living off of welfare, I remember us being fairly poor. Since the men would become the main providers of the household when they came in, they were also the rule-makers. So, growing up, it was their rules I had to strictly follow or else I couldn't live there. It was difficult growing up with them; at times, with some of the rules they made, it felt like they were just abusing their authority. I wasn't able to sing around one of them, I wasn't able to fall asleep on the couch, I had to go to my room if I wanted to rest, it felt as if I wasn't even able to breathe wrong around them or within their presence at times. They just had these rules and justified these rules because of how they were brought up which they would remind me was even more toxic than what I was experiencing. I knew this was all projection but it didn't matter how much I would express this, as I had no idea how to do it in a way where they would listen or even want to question their unjust behaviors. I would look to my mother to stand up for me but whenever she did it would create chaos between her and her husband's relationship, so she would eventually refrain in defending me and just tell me to listen even if the rule was petty. It grew to the point where they both started acting exactly alike and would band together and verbally bully me when I would challenge their behaviors and actions when they didn't seem just or nurturing to or for me in my best interest. They told me I was being disrespectful but I felt they had been showing disrespect to my soul for my entire life. So, I often wondered how they could be angry at me for standing up for myself when I felt as if I had nobody else in my life doing that for me. I thought, at least they have each other, I just have me.

As I grew older, I started noticing my extrasensory abilities developing. I remember one time I asked one of the neighborhood kids if they could see air particles. I started to explain that I just had to focus on the air particles, and then I could see ethereal bodies and symbols. I thought it was something useful I could teach her or show her how to do but instead of being curious she replied, "No, that's weird. You can't see air particles." I tried to explain to her my ability and instead of believing me or wanting to know more about it, she just said, "You're weird, you know?". Another time, when one of my friends' grandmother had passed, I told my friend that I could sense her grandma's presence. At that, she started crying and told me to never say that again. At the time, I didn't really understand why she responded that way to me, because her grandma actually just wanted to send her love. But I came to understand that she couldn't comprehend her presence how I could. I realized that I seemed to be more aware of the emotional and energetic part of life more than the other children too. And so, from there on, I never brought it up again to anybody because I didn't want to be considered even 'weirder' because I was already seen and felt as different and I was already receiving weird and demeaning responses from others without letting them know what I was fully experiencing at depth.

As the years progressed, the wounds and trauma that I had endured from my childhood, interfered with being able to strengthen and progress with my extra sensory abilities. As an adult I came to understand that when you have wounds and extrasensory abilities, you need to know how to effectively process and clear them in order to be able to fully access and learn how to use your inherent gifts. Since I was still developing as a child in the brain and since psychology was still a relatively new science, this information didn't come to me until way later. I think just because of everything that happened to me as a child, others just assumed that I was behaving strangely because of being abused or because of the environment I was born into. So I was already invalidated before I was asking to receive validation from others for how I was perceiving the world.

I would say that most adults in my life growing up who knew my family and my situation, didn't really try to understand me. I believe I was just kind of shunned or looked over because of the fact that I was sexually abused. I vividly recall all the parents in my neighborhood not wanting their kids alone with my mom and me because they didn't trust my mom to watch their children. I could only go to their house and play while their kids weren't allowed to do likewise. That remained the state of affairs for a while. That made me feel a little ostracized because, I would think to myself, why would you use a child's own trauma against them? But that was what I observed my whole life, really. It was heartbreaking and I felt like I was seen as less than human and spent a lot of time alone.

Being empathic as a child, it was not hard for me to be able to attract other children to me. If they didn't know about my past or if they didn't have any knowledge of my past, I was able to connect with others easily. I saw their light, and naturally I was able to reflect it back to them. However, with me being a child I was naïve, and in turn, quick to trust others to have a heart like mine. This would get me into stressful and conflicting situations throughout my life until I would be forced to learn how to discern better as an adult.

One time I was hanging out alongside my cousin with this one boy I had met as a teenager, and we walked with him to his house where his older sibling was smoking marijuana. Later on, to my surprise, my cousin had told on me, like I had been looking to put her in a bad situation. Now, my cousin had been around marijuana her whole life, so I really didn't understand why she would do that unless she wanted to interfere with this connection I was building with this boy. We didn't even go anywhere near the marijuana; we were just conversing with this friend of mine and nothing more. However, she went back and told her mother and then her mother made a huge thing about it and blew it all out of proportion, getting the whole extended family involved and judging me as a trouble maker. When these things would happen, it would feel like a war zone, so much negative energy filled with fear, guilt and shame would be thrown at me through the power of their words and punishments. I would have to sit in the center as they all stood around me as if I was the eye of the storm with their anger and frustration ready to flow out of them at me so they could let go of it for just a moment and not have to carry the weight of it in their chest any longer. So, they could express themselves and be heard in ways they hadn't given themselves permission to access within themselves yet. Again, looking back, this was just another example of a family member taking their frustration and projections out on me, Not realizing that my energy was calling out for it either. They needed to reinforce my differences, my lack of purity from being abused and not understanding or knowing how to respond properly to my highly sensitive nature.

In such circumstances, any person would eventually get frustrated and lash out. I would do my best to stand up for myself but I had no Idea how to emotionally handle myself either as my mother was emotionally avoidant to me. It had been part of my life for so long that it felt like 'normal' for me. But as I matured, I began to see that there was nothing normal about any of this. I remember one time, in my teen years, I did feel suicidal; I had this self-destructive and self-loathing behavior. I just didn't understand why God put me with a family who would not understand me and didn't make sure I felt loved. I believe that the reality of the situation was that most of humanity in general had forgotten how to actually love properly, or at least this part of humanity that I had been placed in.

I just didn't feel like I belonged in this family or in this world. I believed myself to be some kind of burden and that I was just in their way. And I thought to myself that I was just causing more confusion and frustration to them because they lacked the motivation to want to help me and they couldn't figure out how to guide me or react and respond to me so that I could find ways to be content with this reality - this physical reality versus the reality that I felt energetically around me.

Come to think of it, it always felt to me like I came from another place, and I was hoping to find that same place here. But instead, I found a denser reality here, and because of it, I didn't want to be here anymore. I guess I didn't know how to, as this reality made me feel like a fish out of water. I didn't know how to stay with myself through it, as I wasn't receiving enough love outside of myself to really remember how to love myself. Soon, I started to be programmed away from myself. And all those insecurities started to grow and gnaw inside of me because nobody was there to whom I could approach for help. Those who oversaw me just seemed to be in a lot of distress around my presence, and they didn't really understand why so I was usually dismissed or sent to my room to not disrupt them.

It seemed as if they felt as if I was just some annoying energy that they reluctantly had to deal with. As a result, I was passed around a lot from family member to family member in my teenage years because nobody knew how to deal or interact with me. Nor did anybody try to understand me. And the more I got passed around, the more misunderstood I felt, and the more self-loathing I became.

No matter how much I tried, I didn't really understand how to live in this reality when everybody just seemed like they were against me, and it didn't make sense why they would be against me. My mental anguish became so severe that I was hospitalized for about two weeks as a teenager because of my depression.

Eventually, I ended up going through counseling and getting put on antidepressants and other medications. However, none of these modalities worked out for me. The pills didn't take the depression away, they just took everything away and the counseling didn't give me a clear way to operate and/or manage my emotions. In those countless counseling sessions, I could feel everything that my counselors were feeling, so I was able to feel their judgments and their conflicts of interests. I could feel that they were also counseling other kids that maybe were bullies to me, and thus, they weren't clearly trying to empathize with me at all or what I was going through. Rather, they were just trying to find a neutral perspective, which only ended up irritating me. There was no empathy in their counseling; their approach was depersonalized and systematic, similar to a mathematician working on a complex equation, rather than as a person helping a child heal from their trauma. It just seemed like they wanted to give you a label so that they could figure out what kind of medicine to put you on and be done with your case.

If anything, interacting with my counselors took me further away from myself. And that was something that I couldn't let happen because deep inside, I subconsciously knew that I had a larger purpose, my soul knew I had these gifts for a reason and that I would need to use them in the future. I didn't come here to be completely programmed and medicated away from myself. If I had conformed to the system's way of handling behavioral issues at the time, I wouldn't be able to carry out my mission in the future. It was this sense of purpose that allowed me to push through these dark times and aspire toward success.

CHAPTER 3
SEEING AND FEELING LIFE ENERGETICALLY

They say life is nothing more than a product of your thoughts, and this was a universal truth I realized quite early in my life. I could tell that there was something different about me, not only because people reacted to me differently but also because whatever I wanted, it would show up for me just by spending time alone in my room and thinking of it. In other words, I was manifesting as a child and didn't realize that it was happening. Nevertheless, there remained a part of me always reminding me that I was more aware of the latent powers we possess that most others hadn't become consciously aware of. I could feel and see life energetically; I felt a lot of energy behind others' behaviors, and I could see things in nature most just overlooked or didn't even want to bother seeing. I was always hyper aware of the air and the temperature of it, I was always drawn to the light, especially when it flickered along the surface of the water or when it glowed through the leaves of the trees. It was like nature was always showing me its song and dance so I could connect fully to it whenever I needed to re center.

This didn't just happen in nature, it happened all around me all of the time, for an instance, as a child, while riding in a car, I would look at all of the houses that we would drive by and feel into the energy by how they were presenting with the style and color choices of the house. I felt the energies of everything and soon began to understand the interconnectedness in all of it. In a way, I was seeing life in two ways, rather than just the physical and practical reality. Whereas in my world, I was not just paying attention to the physical, I was also paying attention to the emotional, and the metaphysical aspects of – life in many colors and perspectives most around me chose to remain blind to.

Nature and my own inner reflection were where I often returned to when I didn't really know what else to do emotionally. I'll admit I was still confused with the humans around me as I wasn't even sure if I was managing myself properly, as I was led to believe that was what the parents were supposed to be doing so since my parents did their own thing, I just did whatever I had to do to get myself to centered space. My family and those around me didn't really seem to understand self-regulation, they didn't really know how to process their emotions or how to manage their feelings. They either avoided trying to understand themselves more or blamed me for not being able to conform to their way of being. All I could do was just observe, maybe cry if I felt more disconnected from nature than usual which happened often in the winter and be angry that I was living in a reality that I didn't feel my frequency matched to.

And I guess the reason I connected so deeply with nature was because I felt as if it was the closest thing to my natural frequency because it was nature who helped me through some very isolating and confusing times throughout my childhood. There were a lot of aspects surrounding my existence that I just didn't know what to make of. And I didn't have anybody around me that was similar to me that could help guide me. So, the only thing I could do was just return back to nature.

Thus, whenever I was confused about something or felt like something was unjust, I would go visit nature and feel out all its energies to go into a more centered state. I guess I loved nature because, compared to my 'human reality,' it was more harmonious, more tranquil, more forgiving, and more loving. Truly, the contrast is stark: in nature, everything is integrated beautifully, but with humanity, we're all just so destructive towards each other and to nature.

I could just feel. I could feel a lot; I could sense when somebody needed to be loved and cared for. I could sense so much and so many things. I just didn't know what, at that point in my life, I didn't know what to do with all that information.

And so, because I grew up in what seemed a largely different reality than most, a part of me was free and still connected enough to see the magic in reality; I didn't have to always see it as depressing. The sunlight always brought me into this space. I subtly noticed this as a child but I somehow knew that it was going to be a long time before I would truly understand the importance of it.

Ironically, even though a part of me could tell I was different, another part of me thought of myself as just like everyone else. I continued to believe that I was normal and others, too, could feel the same way I did. Thus, often, I ended up getting confused whenever I responded to something based on the physical and the energetic components of it, and the other person, not being able to receive my perspectives, wouldn't understand why I was responding the way I did, whether it was positive or negative. Often people mistook my way of seeing things as strange or knowing it all, but, in reality, it was more just like energetically assessing things. I was constantly trying to figure out what was in alignment outside of nature with me as a child, but lacking a proper understanding of what I was doing, I often ended up getting frustrated, especially since I was constrained in my ability and in my rights as a child.

Though, in hindsight, I realized that my relative isolation only enhanced my spiritual and sensory abilities. I would astral travel a lot as a child; I would go into deep meditation before bed, and I would just travel in my sleep because I didn't like how heavy the reality felt where I was physically living. And then I would go and spend time in nature, discovering all these little spots that harbored its secrets and connecting with all the living beings that resided within them.

Of course, I could not ignore the physical reality I resided in; I still had my social and familial life to attend to. So, by the time I was in my adolescent years, I really started worrying about acceptance. And that's when I fell into the control matrix of programs and expectations and superficial commitments in an attempt at trying to fit in. But, to be honest, my whole childhood was nothing less than an uphill battle of finding acceptance because my parents moved to different towns and states every couple of years and I had to start over a lot. I wasn't able to ground long enough to understand myself fully through crucial developmental years and it was hard to find others to relate to or that could understand how to communicate with me. But, looking back, I guess the real kicker of all of this is that I wasn't really meant to be understood. We have our purpose, and the universe conspires to prepare us for it.

As a child, I was just meant to study the darkness so that I could help bring light to it as an adult and to eventually help repair it and mend it through specially analyzed healing protocols to help remove it from the collective consciousness so that we may continue to evolve towards our highest possible time-lines,

At the time, I didn't realize this. But it was the true essence of my personal energy that was not matching up with my physical reality that made it terribly unjust for me to experience. As such, I would react riotously when my parents would be in a power struggle with me, for the very reasons of their energies not aligning with mine. I could feel when the energies were deceptive, unjust, or manipulative. I could sense energy shifts and the negativity behind their behaviors. The biggest indicators were the eyes; they would have an egotistical visage rather than one soulful. I could tell when somebody was operating from the soul or the ego.

Recalling one particular instance, one time when I was with my aunt at a store, and she was irritated by me because, like any other young child, I was asking for everything. So, what she did was she went and bought something for my brother and looked at me with a malicious grin. In my mind, I was like, *'Why would you do this? Why would you purposely buy something for my brother and shove it in my face? Because I'm just curious and want to ask for something?'* It was like she was trying to break me and proceeded to do so in such a messed-up way. I was like, *'that's not how you're gonna get me to stop asking for something, you know? That's just gonna make me not like you and actually cause more of a rift between our relationships than it is going to be.'*

To me, that felt so petty yet cruel to come from someone who was watching me and had the job of keeping me safe as, I just felt that as an adult and as an annoyed reaction to a child's curiosity and behavior. I called her Tremaine, the stepmother from Cinderella, because that's what her energy reminded me of. It was disrespectful, but in my childlike mind I was speaking of the energy but I did express it in a way that probably seemed cruel to her.

I was just so mad that she did that because it was like she was trying to show me that I had to be silent in order to get rewarded. And I knew that, that wasn't right. Even if I was being annoying. I felt that was more damaging than her just not getting either one of us anything. Obviously, she did get mad at me for calling her the ugly step mother, but even more importantly, it upset her ego. Hence, she punished me by not ever watching me again, & telling my mother which meant that I would be punished at home by her too.

Of course, being young and innocent, I couldn't fully interpret what I was seeing; only now did I realize the full picture. Sensing such behavior, my younger self would be puzzled with questions: *What the heck is going on? Why are you coming at me in a very malicious way? Why would you do that? How is that going to help me become a better person? Isn't the whole point of what you're supposed to be doing here is you're supposed to be helping?*

At that point in my life, I felt like everybody should be trying to help humanity for the greater good, but they weren't.

Everything seemed to revolve around self-interest and self-gain; the survival of the fittest with every man for himself. Feeling more interconnected with the energy of the plants and the earth I wasn't living like that at all, but everybody else around me was, and that remained the root of so many conflicts I had with the reality around me.

To a deep feeling person like me, it just all felt too horrible because it wasn't just me such behavior was causing trauma to, but so many others that I knew. I watched it happen to all my friends and siblings. The way I would see adults behave with each other and with children was as if we were in a warzone and the children were prisoners of war, for the most part, not having any rights to even stand up for themselves. Not being loved fully or nurtured properly. Thus, I could clearly see that they were damaging them not only by not allowing them to have a voice but also by limiting their autonomy.

However, I didn't lose hope. There were genuine moments of positivity when I would feel loved, or the adults would show true kindness. Though I could sense it lacking in my parents and family, in that of my friends' families, I could feel that there was more commitment, loyalty, dedication, and unconditional love inherent in their familial links. It showed me that the cycle of suffering wasn't set in stone but could be changed, that you could choose how you wanted to view reality and exist in this reality regardless of your past circumstances. You would just need to change environments.

And naturally, As I grew older, I was drawn towards such others that preferred the natural biorhythms of the earth as they were more energetically in alignment with me. Having the right company and influences are so very important in not only how you are eventually molded into as an adult but also can act as a safeguard against all the negative energy that surrounds you daily and may seek to only drain you of your spirit.

CHAPTER 4
SEEKING ACCEPTANCE

As a child, I tried my best to stay true to myself by honoring and valuing the fact that I was different, that is, until I got to an age where being different started to cause too much disruption which got me bullied, shunned, criticized, and looked down on by others outside of my family and within my community. I believe this phase started during my preteen years when I was around 13 years old. It seemed as if I just attracted a lot of negative attention towards me in a lot of different ways. So, I was bullied really badly in high school, and it made my life just incredibly miserable. Of course, I wasn't passive about it; I tried to stand up for myself, but it always seemed to make things worse. Nevertheless, I was never the one to accept being a pushover, but I still tried. But eventually, it wore on me to the point where I just stopped allowing myself to be me. The constant bullying, harassment, intimidation, and everything…it was all too much. I didn't want to deal with the hassle of getting picked on, ridiculed, and hurt.

And so, I started trying to just blend in a little bit more and fake interest in whatever was popular with everyone else. For instance, I started to try to jump on the fashion trends so that I could be perceived as 'normal.' Because if I was going to stand out, I needed them to think I was standing out because of the brands that they approved of. It was a disguise for the most part. It wouldn't be dishonest to say that the real me was viewed as some kind of threat to classmates and or others outside of my family. At the time, I didn't really understand which of the reasons why they felt this way towards me, especially if they didn't know my past. It was frustrating and also very exhausting to work through.

My frequency told them that they were not in alignment with me or in some cases, their true selves. Not understanding how to explain this to anyone, I would try my best to ignore the distress signals I would receive. It didn't help either that the whole point of having this ability was to be able to show them how their ego was controlling their minds and behaviors through their nervous system and that they were no longer connected to their heart space. As I explained in my previous chapter, people just don't take it well when you call them out on that, there's a program of insecurity embedded for fear of not being perfect. To me I thought I was letting them know that they had other rooms with lights to explore. Yet again, I didn't know this at the time. Rather, I just continued to revert back to the familiar feelings of being untouchable, undeserving, or unworthy. Naturally, this greatly devastated my self-esteem.

In my attempts to seek acceptance, I stopped paying attention to my gifts and to the extra information that I was receiving from others around. I just kind of ignored or blocked them mostly, only paid attention to them when I absolutely had to. I tried to make myself appear as unremarkable and 'normal' as possible. I had to hide in the system that was created by the egoic mindset in order to not be seen, heard, or felt in the wrong way. I had to conform as much as I could to gain the knowledge and the acceptance that I needed to continue to make sense of this strange and confusing life which I was having a hard time obtaining by this point on my own as my days grew busier with schooling and jobs.

Yet, even as my outer self-blended in, my spirit remained as curious and free as ever. If anything, my attempt at fitting in led me on a journey to understand myself even more fully.

I continued to educate myself on a variety of different subjects: psychology, philosophy, law, history, theology, world religion, quantum mechanics, and more. I just educated myself on everything possible to try to understand more about myself subconsciously and fit in consciously. So, my soul was doing all this work in the background, making sure that I had the information that was needed to be prepared when the time was right to step into my light.

But the part of me that was the shell, the conscious part, couldn't be blinded to the misery I went through; I didn't know how to process it fully even after coming out of my educational years. And so after, I had to confront all those past memories of suffering that I had held on to in order to make it through to the end of those chapters. It took probably about two decades to make peace with my past trauma, repressed feelings, limiting beliefs, unnecessary fears, and all that I endured. To an extent, college, too, was difficult because I still had to deal with intimidation by some professors because they didn't like how I challenged their perspectives which I felt like, was too closed off. The more I tried not to, I just couldn't help myself when it came to correcting the riotously wrong. I would get so upset with how they were testing us because they weren't allowing us room to grow, expand, or evolve. They were charging us so much money, yet only stifling our growth – how could I not get upset?

I remember one time I had a religion professor who gave us the assignment to write a paper on different religions and what we felt about them. I thought the assignment was a little boring, so I went ahead and just created a whole new perspective on religion out of all the religions that I had learned about. The paper I had wrote pondered *"What if you combine evolution with the beliefs and concepts in the Bible?"* For instance, if Earth was made in seven days, how did all this time of evolution just happen in that timeframe? She gave me a D on the paper. Upset and also curious, I asked to speak with her. She took me to her office, where I asked her, "Why are you giving me a D on this paper? I spent about four hours on it."

She replied, "Because you can't combine evolution with the Bible."

At that, I just looked at her and asked, "Why can't you?"

"Because it's not allowed," she answered.

And so, I asked, "Why isn't it allowed?"

"You just can't do it," was her response.

I just continued to look at her before speaking, "You know what? I'm just gonna go to the Dean about this because I feel like that's wrong. I don't feel like this is right."

At that, she said, "Can you give me your paper back really quick?"

At her request I gave her my paper, and she changed my grade from a D to a B+. And then, I ended up getting an A in the class.

I don't know what happened. But it wasn't the first time that weird stuff like that would occur with professors. It happened when I would stand up for myself and challenge whom I felt had this ego that was blocking the ability for both of our minds to be able to expand and evolve.

Looking back, it just seemed like I was admired by those who helped educate me for my strength but also criticized for my way of thinking. It's almost like I noticed that glitch in the flow of life, you know, when they did that kind of stuff, and I got mad at them for it. I let them know that it was not right; sometimes, they would lash back at me, and then sometimes, they would just give me what I wanted so I wouldn't bring to light what they were doing. I was still having a hard time just having a 'normal' life because I was moving through life so differently that what I was programed and conditioned to survive in, it was a little nauseating at times as it felt as if I would have to switch back and forth from different ways of existing depending on the environment that I was in. I was obtaining a lot of knowledge to help make more sense of things in a way that could help me gear myself better in positively changing the world around me.

CHAPTER 5
CONFUSION

Being an introvert since childhood, I spent most of my life observing people, analyzing the possibility of different scenarios, and predicting future outcomes. I was also extroverted because my energy spoke for me & drew a lot of attention towards me which was overwhelming especially if I wasn't sure what was showing up in front of me or how to mentally prepare or protect myself from it. Since it usually didn't pair up well for too long with me. Perhaps, this was the reason that I had a hard time trusting people and getting close to them. Whenever I was around a lot of people or part of a group conversation, there was something that greatly disturbed me. As if there was an unsolvable puzzle, it interrogated me time and again about why people do not say what they feel. Why do their words showcase the kind of energy that does not really belong to them? Why do they hide things and bury them in some corner of their heart, knowing that this can hurt them more in the long run? Deep inside my heart, I tried to avoid the reality of not being able to blend well but I would naively walk into situations out of curiosity or stability that would later blow up in my face unexpectedly. So, I was forced to engage in conversations that I wasn't even wanting to have. Conversations that create an image about something that does not exist as a universal truth. Yet, I had to fake myself and project what I felt was a misunderstood image of myself to others just so I could feel accepted and validated.

Lost amidst this self-deception, as I looked inward, I noticed I had stopped feeling into the energies around me and checking in with my intuition. I realized that, by seeking acceptance outside of myself, it made me worry more about how others perceived me. I started losing touch with my extrasensory abilities as I started to experiment with alcohol and carried on with activities like binge drinking on the weekends with friends as a teenager and trying to go with the flow of the programs everyone was operating from & saw fit to follow as a majority.

I started engaging in gossip and became my own worst enemy. I began to notice that the same feelings I detested in others – insecurities, jealousy, and envy – were now surfacing within me. My wounds were hidden behind the mask I was trying to wear in a world I didn't feel like I belonged in, and, in the process, I was slowly tearing myself apart. It was pure hell. I didn't even know who I was anymore.

My priorities changed to what I thought would gain me more acceptance from others. I feel like I tried too hard because of how much I hated standing out and possibly having to face rejection, being shunned, or being bullied. It was like I was trying to live in a world I wasn't able to stay emotionally invested in because it was not the world that I truly wanted to be in, it was not the world where I felt like my best self in.

In hindsight, it was a world I created worse than the one I sought to avoid. It was like by going against my own true nature I amplified the hell of where the world resided outside of me to begin with. I would have frequent panic and anxiety attacks because I was no longer taking care of myself and checking in with myself intuitively like I did naturally as a child. I spent less time in nature, and I noticed a decline in my intuition.

I believe this all started to worsen when my grandmother died at the age of 12. My grandmother seemed to be the only person in the world who understood me on a soul level, and when she died, a beautiful part of me in the forefront of my consciousness went with her for a while too. I remember experiencing depression for the first time since my attachment to her was so strong. It was also my first experience with death, so I was mad at the universe for taking the person who resonated with me most! Maybe I even lost some faith and fell into the logical, practical mindset that restricted me from being able to use my extrasensory abilities openly and freely.

I went in and out of engaging with creating cycles of suffering during that time frame, and I knew I was creating horrible karma for myself. I was in conflict with myself over this for a long part of my life as I couldn't bear living in this reality because it felt like hell.

What I didn't realize was that in the background, my soul was setting me up to find my way out of it. Even though I wasn't conscious of it, my light led the way in the background taking notes, educating myself out of the confusion to help build a better understanding of it, and helping me spiritually reconnect with every lesson I had learned to help create a better world for me. As I look back, I was studying the darkness to later bring light to it. However, at the time, I thought I was in hell and only making matters worse for myself. It made me feel so guilty, shameful, and frustrated.

These frequencies almost paralyzed me, but I struggled on. A part of me knew I needed to experience it in order to gain the empathy, compassion, and insight so I could eventually help others find their way out of it in the future. I somehow knew that I was here to be a game changer, that I was meant to understand this existence to help others understand it too. Of course, I ran into so many roadblocks along the way, but I refused to give up and just kept going through them. I didn't always approach these roadblocks emotionally correctly, but I definitely left an impact on making sure that change needed to be made. I always let whoever was abusing their power know what they were doing was wrong while usually pointing the finger at me to correct my behavior to conform to their expectations first, and I was not the type to quietly tolerate it. And this was especially true if the flawed system they sought to push on me didn't have an ethical foundation of unconditional love and interconnectedness that resonated with the natural laws for the greater good of all.

In my journey towards self-transformation, I wasn't always my best self, but at least my worst self was learning, growing, and healing to become a better version in the future. I never meant to hurt anyone emotionally or energetically, not to justify hurtful behaviors but a part of me somehow knew that I would experience the hell of it all in order to help myself understand it better.

As time passed, I continued to observe and react and record all behaviors which helped me to shift my perspective about others and gave me further insight into how to bring about healing and change in myself and in them. I set out a mission for myself to always help others heal, help them speak up, and communicate for their own personal well-being and sovereignty. Whether it was with a relationship or a business venture, communication was the key. I wanted them to feel heard and speak the words right from their souls. I wanted real connections not superficial connections. Because I could feel it, I felt like I was obligated to bring it to the attention of others before they let it start to cause damage. It was not that I was trying to interfere in their life, I was trying to find a way to express how their repressed emotions were harming them; I was just making an effort to help them understand themselves better by helping them see their blockage trapped inside of them. I noticed then that until we embrace these pains & these hurts and we acknowledge them, and talk about them, how will we ever heal from them as a collective force? How will this unify us to work together in peace with balance and harmony?

Unfortunately, this didn't go as I had planned, the more I made others whom I was close to speak up about what was bothering them, the more they started to dislike me. While I was trying to help them align their mind with their body and soul like nature had taught me, and help them see the emotions come before the lies that they were deceiving themselves with, they would always lash out at me and want to grow distant from me. However, the pain I endured as many walked away from me, most do come back around to apologize to me, throughout the years. I appreciate this but I also grieve the time together that has been lost as a result of choosing to stay in pain rather than deepen the connection to self, face their blockages, work through things together and choose to love rather than stay angry and hurt with one another.

However, despite all of the criticism, I still continued to try to helping others speak up, hold space for themselves, help them communicate with themselves about things that are hard to talk about and work through the stuff that have been buried inside of their hearts for so long that they have unknowingly blocked themselves from being able to fully experience happiness or even access their heart space. When a human can no longer access their heart space, they will not be able to access their true essence and will not be reminded as often or as loudly of how to express it, nurture it or naturally return to it. This will over time wear on the body as the true-life force is no longer being fed and the nervous system is fed instead for survival mode, interfering with a person's ability to heal or resolve blocked energy. This will eventually break the body, the mind and the spirit over time and we will begin to suffer from mental and physical ailments because of it.

I believe I will always continue to grow more into the awareness and depth of this nature and to become more of this person I am today. Because not only did I understand this type of blockage, I had experienced what was causing it in so many ways through feeling into the projections of their pain as a child and how I had also reluctantly discovered how painful it was to project it out onto others as well as I grew into adulthood. Neither of these experiences were pleasant and they caused more unpleasant experiences for myself so I had to find a way to make it healthier and more loving all while growing into an adult and learning how to navigate my intuition and emotions better as well as learn how to get a better handle on the extra energetic stimuli I was picking up on.

CHAPTER 6
EDUCATION

Before I pursued my higher education, I felt a need to get my life in order. It was all in chaos; I felt like I didn't really understand what the world was trying to do because the information I was receiving, and the information I was trying to give out, were not in alignment with each other. I was just so confused, with my mind racing with questions: Why is everyone so hurtful to each other? Why are these systems so restricted? Why can't we just relax instead of partaking in and sustaining this made-up system of social oppression?

I needed to figure out how to push through this psychological warfare that I seemed to be caught up in. Similar to many young people in the States, I went into the military. Before I would study higher education, I had decided that it was best that I geared up to strengthen my psychological state, and hence I enlisted in the Marine Corps. However, I found out very quickly that my body could not support the combat training. Nevertheless, I remained there long enough to make it through boot camp and learn how to overcome the worst of psychological warfare with practice. Despite my physical shortcomings, I wanted to make it through, even if it meant breaking everything inside of me. I had to figure out how to make it through it, and I did! I made it through the Bootcamp. And that achievement showed me I was mentally tough enough and that I had it in me to overcome mental challenges; all that was needed was for me to not doubt myself and stay with myself.

Still, military life was taking a toll on me physically, and hence it was not where I could stay for long. I just kept breaking my feet in the military. And eventually, if you seriously injure yourself too many times, they just tell you that you need to find a new career, and they help you go back into civilian life. They gave me money to go to higher education, and that allowed me to enroll debt free in nursing school. At the time, the reason I chose nursing was that, while I was in the Naval Hospital being treated for my conditions, I bonded well with the nurses and the doctors there. They were really kind to me, and I really liked how they wanted to help me, so I was inspired to do the same with others; I wanted to help people heal,

But coming back, after I went and enrolled in the nursing program, doing all the prerequisites for it, one of the nursing instructors came to me at the end of the semester and told me she felt I should transfer out to a four-year and become a doctor instead. She told me she felt certain I could go further if I wanted to. Encouraged by her advice, I made a move and got a transfer scholarship to Le Moyne College, a Jesuit college. The reason I chose it was because they were tolerant of all religions, and there you could opt to take seminars in more art fields like literature, history, philosophy, and religion. So, with my life experience, on top of these seminars I took along with my curriculum which helped me see the bigger picture, I was going into molecular biology to try to get into the Physician Assistant Program. So, I went, and I just started educating myself on many topics that I felt would aid in my discoveries and I learned a lot of very useful information to help me understand the inner workings of the microcosm better. I didn't realize how significant this would become as I would later be able to pair up with the macrocosm to find similarities and commonalities that interconnected them together in beautiful and healing ways. However, later on, as I dove into subjects such as organic chemistry, I was appalled to find that the way they were testing us felt so restrictive. To recall my own personal experience, for instance, it was literally interfering with my ability to even concentrate on why I was doing it, to begin with. The way it was taught was simply unhelpful and non-intuitive to the student. I'd study for weeks and weeks and weeks, and I still wouldn't be able to make much sense of it, and I couldn't figure out why.

Eventually, I began to question myself and ask if I really was academically inclined enough to go through the program. In hindsight, now understand that the real problem was with the way that my brain was being tested didn't match the way my brain likes to learn and take in information, also intuitively the system and subjects felt off to me.

Our education system in some aspects doesn't tell us intelligence or even our aptitude towards a certain subject, but rather our skills in memorization of theory. I noticed that in my experiences the testing was not effective for impacting critical skills that would actually be beneficial in real-life situations for me. And then there is the dilemma with our teachers and professors – many of them just weren't really interested in helping us learn, nor did they showcase a passion to help students learn the material effectively. At times, it was almost like they were testing to taunt us and weed us out.

Since I was a full-time student trying to find my way through life without much familial support, I still had to pay for a place to live, so I took up an overnight job at a local mental health support agency. We would work with individuals that had just been released from the psychiatric hospitals and help them integrate back into civilization. Since I did mostly overnights, I would monitor night and morning medications and answer any distress calls that the clients had during those time frames. Over time while monitoring medications I would notice that most of the clients would be taken off of a specific controlled medication and then switched over to another. This seemed to happen a little too often as I noticed the same clients going on and off medications at the same time. It gave off an energy as if controlled trials were being done to see how these clients would respond to the changes in medicine. It was my job to observe and log any strange or harmful side effects that would occur. Although I have no proof that this was actually happening, it gave me an uncomfortable feeling knowing that I might be participating in something unethical without pepper consent. Not only did it seem like the medical system was treating the clients as guinea pigs I noticed that they would come into the program on a couple of medications from the hospital and leave the program taking a whole cup full of medication, sometimes up to 20 different pills. To me this didn't seem healthy or even ethical as I watched how the medication over time caused weight gain, damaged their body and changed their entire personalities. I felt helpless to the things I was able to pick up on and do nothing about so I knew that when pre-med curriculum started interfering with my ability to function, I was making the right choice to not become a western medical practitioner.

Realizing that there was no way for me to change how the education curriculum for the pre medicine system worked, I switched over to psychology two years after trying to work through that, and boy, did I make the right decision. The change I felt overnight was massive. My anxiety and depression started to fade away, and I started to feel myself heal. Furthermore, psychology was a course that really clicked with me naturally. I had plenty of life experiences to help me understand the diagnosis and the explanations of how trauma and conditioning can affect human behavior immensely. In psychology most of the classes were discussion based and also relied on written reports to measure the understanding of the material. I felt as if this was a better way for me to learn and combine what I had learned so far from experience with the knowledge I was gaining from these courses. I remember writing a report in my life span class on what the statistics displayed as the long-term damage on overall psychological and physical health of someone who had experienced the hardships that I had gone through as a child. After starting to do the research for this paper it became evident that I was an outlier to what the information was presenting. To my surprise, after experiencing childhood sexual abuse and domestic violence, the overall outcome for anyone was bleak. The report was upsetting as I saw that those who had experienced similar traumas were likely to be obese, live shorter lifespans, suffer from anxiety and depression and be unable to interact healthily with others due to developed psychological conditions and various personality disorders that developed along the way. I remember feeling my throat lock up as I cried about the results I was studying and I remember thinking to myself that I really needed to find a way to help others through these types of suffering as it was not fair or right for them to become lost inside their own mind because of someone else's projections and violating behaviors. In that moment, I vowed to be a voice for those who had not yet found their way back to theirs. I wanted to find new ways to bring us back to our heart and to be able to feel safe in our body again.

For a long time, I had been really confused about the way humans were operating and interacting with one another and why we continued to operate the way we were operating. At first, I opted to learn primate behavior just so I could maybe better understand our instinctual behavior based on the theory of evolution. I wanted to understand why adult humans behaved the way they did when I was a child and maybe even find answers to how to work through some of my own unique behaviors which I felt were instinctually different. I even reached out to a school in the Congo, and I learned Sign Language to be able to communicate with them. However, later on, I woke up one morning and just realized that my calling was more towards higher consciousness; as in healing our way back to it. It was almost like I woke up having a "knowing" that higher consciousness was more instinctual on a soul and human level rather than primate behavior which was believed in theory to prelude human behavior. I knew at that moment that I was meant to study higher consciousness. To be more specific, to study the future of psychology: the ontology of spirituality, religion, and belief systems.

So, I looked up some professions that would help me study the bridge that connected the mind, the body, and the soul, and it led me to the field of acupuncture.

It was, at that point, in my mind that I decided Acupuncture was going to be it. The career had a good income, and it aligned with the principles and beliefs that I was trying to further advance in. With my decision made, I went to the Dean of Psychology to ask her for a letter of recommendation to the Finger Lakes School for Acupuncture in upstate NY. I remember her asking me, "Why'd you want to switch from instinctual behavior to acupuncture? I told her all that had transpired that manifested in me making a move and discovering my true calling. Hearing this, she then expressed to me that she felt as if I was probably a "starseed."

Now, I had never prior heard that term in my entire life. And it sounded *extraterrestrial.* I wasn't really sure how to respond to the word or the idea of it being a being from another world, but she was the Dean of the Psychology Department at Le Moyne college, and I was pretty sure that she knew something I didn't at that point. Thus, I trusted that what she told me would, at some point in my life, make sense.

On her recommendation, I also signed up for some "starseed" newsletter that I would get emails about and sometimes read. Fast forward some five or six years later, I looked at one such email, and all of a sudden, it triggered the activation of my third eye. So, it was that email that helped initiate further analysis of where I was trying to go. Slowly, all that I had learned and experienced was starting to make sense – the vision of my life's purpose was becoming clearer.

CHAPTER 7
PRACTICE

Entering the professional world is certainly a big transition in one's life. When we enter, we are quite idealistic or structured and have quite rosy pictures of how things are. Little are we prepared for the corruption and greed that pervades the business world. It doesn't help either that we often do not challenge it when we should. When I graduated from my master's program in acupuncture, I was basically told I had to only be an acupuncturist a certain way. So, I went out and sought employment under a couple of other types of practitioners. Truth be told, working under them, I didn't feel like they valued me as a person or practitioner; it honestly felt as if money was the main focus. Not wanting to feel like another form of income for them, I ended up going into private practice, and, to my surprise, my patients ended up following me.

In hindsight, I can understand why that happened. I didn't realize how good I was at my job in helping people feel better and heal until I saw the overwhelming response of positivity coming from all of the patients that I was working with. They were just really happy to have me as a healing support system and were coming from a heart-centered space. It was a connection I hadn't experienced before in school or with my family; it felt authentic. It felt like I was naturally following my path.

And so, I started really wanting to make sure that I was offering as much as I could for them because they were trusting me to take care of them. Although it felt like a bold move to go out on my own, I knew I needed to stand up for myself and for my patients, it was hard to focus on the practice the way I truly wanted to because I was under pressure from other practitioners in the area constantly trying to either pick me apart to mutual patients or trying to dim my light. As hurtful as it was, I did not let myself become discouraged. They tried everything they could to stay in control and make me out to be less valuable than I was. It was disheartening and disappointing to see adults in the healing professions treating me this way but I vowed to myself that I would learn from the experience and do better.

Initially, running my own practice was challenging because I had to go blindly into structures of the business world, which were really cold and ruthless. With money being the most motivating factor. Since I was able to pick up on this, I was worried that by following these structures I would fall into the trap too so I came up with other ways to make the experience more centered on their treatment plans rather than how much it was going to cost so they would be able to see their healing experience as an investment in their overall health and wellbeing rather than paying for a service that they weren't sure would work. I made sure my prices were affordable and that I wasn't taking more from them than I was able to return with my current abilities and skills. Because of the structure of the business world and because of judgements that the other practitioners placed on me, the whole business side of the healing practice was getting really stressful. Hence, to keep myself calm, I started meditating a lot and I started seeking out other complementary therapies within the field of holistic healing; I noticed that, with acupuncture, there wasn't just a physical element to it but also an emotional one. In addition, there was also a lifeforce activation aspect of acupuncture.

And so, I started delving into all sorts of emotional aspects. I took a bunch of seminars on emotional and shamanic healing through acupuncture. I then took some workshops on esoteric acupuncture to work on and learn more about the energy systems of the body known as the chakras. I educated myself on how to meditate and how to work with the chakras while meditating. I felt as if I was on a roll! I also began my Reiki certifications to try to understand the world that we could feel but not see. I just wanted to get to the bottom of all of the hurtful, deceptive and manipulative behaviors that cause us harm because, throughout my life, I never felt like they were necessary. I still didn't understand why these types of behaviors had to exist. Especially after seeing and experiencing the aftermath from myself and others that I was working with, and it really made me ponder what I could continue to do to help prevent these harmful implications that all of it was causing to the human mind, body and spirit.

As my knowledge and awareness increased, so did I begin to see more patterns around me – of how everything seemed to be strangely interconnected. I started to see where people were missing their spark and where people were operating off of similar programs. I could now sense if a patient was going to receive well to acupuncture or not because of how open they were to want to receive it.

The pursuit of my passion for helping others did, however, cause me to neglect some of my own needs. As I was working really hard to build a practice, I was having a really hard time finding authentic connections with partners; I couldn't understand what was going in this aspect of my life because it seemed as if we had all forgotten how to love and be loved in a healthy interpersonal relationship; it did not appear to be unconditional

– it had to make sense, physically and financially, in order for a connection to even be established.

And, to me, that just felt confusing. I had always felt that when you were operating from your heart center and when you're being authentic and transparent, that your connection will be so strong and deep that abundance would show up as a result of the union of two souls that wanted to build and create together. Maybe this was naive of me but it was an inherent knowing that I had been carrying my entire life but could not and had not seen play out physically in front of me. And that is what I think everybody needs to realize: once you figure out your rhythm, who you are, what you are, why you're here, and you actually start to wake up and step in alignment with your destiny. Basically, everything you've ever wished for or dreamed of is just going to show up for you, because you're calling it to you, because you just have this knowing that you deserve it and that you're worthy of it and that it's a part of you already. It's almost like your whole life flashes through you before you are born and then after you are born you are expected to figure out how to get to the finish line of your highest possible timeline. But everything in front of you is not representative of where you are trying to go so you have to listen to this other part of you that you can't physically see to help guide you there regardless of what's physically happening around you as you grow, as you learn and as you go through the chapters of your life. You have to keep going inside and asking for more pieces to the puzzle so that you can stay on the right trajectory, so that you don't make things harder for yourself, so that you learn to find patients and safety and trust and acceptance within yourself in order to get to where you know you want to go. It sometimes feels like we are searching for gold and that the gold can only be found in this physical reality by studying the map of your soul.

I knew that what I was tapping into within myself was very beautiful and real, but what I didn't know was how to get myself into alignment to prove it to others that it was within them too. So, I just stayed open to the learning process and I kept trying to get closer to myself each day.

The thing is, people aren't going to hold you credible unless you give them the proof. Acupuncture didn't have much scientific proof according to the way the Western world measures things and operates. Therefore, I knew I was going to have to give them a live transformational view somehow. And that *somehow,* I believed I would find it by continuing to study until the hidden facts themselves were revealed.

I truly felt it was my life's mission to discover those hidden facts so I could finally be in a position to truly help others heal physically, mentally, and spiritually. I would have so many clients come in and just cry on the table to me as soon as I put the acupuncture needles in, because they had nowhere else to cry or express their hurt. They needed a safe place to heal, to be themselves, and to have some respite from the world that was feeling so repressive to them. They were tired of having to hold up to so many standards, expectations and rules outside of the treatment room in order to actually be who they were, and it was making them sick. As the seasons were shifting, their conditions would flare up because their body was already trying to sustain from so much emotional weight that they were carrying, which I perceived as a result just from having to live a life that didn't fall into alignment with who they truly were. Because they grew into who they thought they were supposed to be in order to conform and to feel safe, rather than grow and create their life in a way that honored who they truly were and wanted to openly express themselves as.

They were living this way because they felt like they had to, and because of this they were no longer enjoying their life. They were losing their spark. They were living in survival mode and following expectations and obligations that were going against the part of them that fed them life. They would express these pains to me with so much regret and shame. I could see and feel how hurt everybody silently was and how lost everybody around me was, but they couldn't admit it out loud to anyone but me it seemed. They didn't understand why they were feeling this way and why their body was reacting the in ways it was as a result of it. And then it hit me: I found that this problem was also hindering aspects of myself too.

My meditations and my relentless pursuit of learning more allowed me to see what I was, what I was lacking, and where I needed to pay more attention. Within the vastness of my own expansiveness and my inner universe, I started to figure out how to articulate this to everybody else so that they could discover this as well and not feel lost in their minds, or confused about their body anymore, so that they could feel good again, and nurture their life force, so they could move closer to living their best life again.

And it was another sign, during these moments in my life that I knew that I was in the right profession. I was someone who was helping others heal, providing them a safe space and giving them permission to be themselves, showing them how to connect back to themselves and helping them nurture these aspects of themselves so that they could find their way back to feeling whole again. This is what I wish I could have done for my parents, for my family. I wanted to understand their pain and suffering and I wanted to help them see their own light. I knew I had the ability as a child but nobody around me would listen. Now I was being heard and I was able to express myself better to be able to articulate my perception of reality better as I was seen as valid and credible in the eyes of my patients and I valued their respect and trust, so it fed my passion to make a difference and it just drove me to do better for myself, for them and for humanity.

Especially in uncertain and stressful times, it's very important that we all feel safe, supported, and loved so we can heal from all the wounds and scars that we have accumulated. Unless we heal, we are not going to be able to make the best authentic decisions for ourselves, because the trauma blocks us, the limiting beliefs hold us back and the unnecessary fears paralyze us, eventually fading out the spark of our life force and our bodies' willingness to live a higher quality of life. We stop believing in ourselves and we lose interest in trying to help ourselves and we fade out with our body to follow and we don't get to live up to our highest quality or potential because we had either forgotten how or were never taught how to love ourselves, how properly connect with ourselves and/or how to take care of ourselves.

"Measured against eternity, our time on earth is just a blink of an eye, but the consequences of it will last forever." – Rick Warren.

CHAPTER 8
THE EVOLUTION OF THE HEALER IN LIGHT WORK

With my private practice and having gone through my journey of self-realization, I felt that now things were truly aligning, and I was able to fulfill my life purpose. While I was treating the patients, I saw a really positive response from the healing process that I was helping to facilitate for them. However, I genuinely felt there was more I could do; I just didn't know exactly what. So, I started immersing myself in other studies, such as esoteric. While I could tell, having a background in psychology, that the emotional state was like any kind of physical ailment, I was picking up that it was being derived from an energetic ailment first and, over time, if it did not properly tended to, it would eventually turn into a physical ailment. So, when they say, "stress wears on the body," that would be like the energetic component wearing on the body over time.

Under this context, I wanted to explore the emotional body a little bit more, as well as the lifeforce – the actual lifeforce within people to help them heal and feel their best. So, I started studying and practicing esoteric studies for acupuncture. In addition, I got into meditation, started researching it, and went to meditation and feeling workshops. I was eager to learn more and discover more about this realm of human existence. I also obtained a certification and was attuned in Reiki during this timeframe.

I was advancing quickly in my meditation practices to where I would get into a trance-like state and have images and visuals present to me in my mind's eye. It started as colors and then slowly worked its way into images and eventually what seemed like small movie clips. I talked to the meditation instructor about it, and I feel like she kind of knew I was starting to go a little bit deeper into my 'gifts.' She recognized where I was at in my process and encouraged me to keep meditating.

Relating to my gifts, I recall going to a national forest in upstate New York this one time. It was a beautiful summer day, and I was really just exploring it. My travel through the woodland really started getting magical for me; I was visibly noticing that reality was a little bit more expansive than I thought it was. I found a bunch of turkey feathers where turkeys roosted then I came to this big clearing into what looked like wild fields being grazed by cattle.

Taking in the atmosphere around me, I sat down, and I soon began to feel like the whole forest was like talking to me; the way the leaves were like blowing; the way the sun rays were dancing off of everything; the way the multitude of its inhabitants called out their presence. I just started to get really in tune with it, and then, as I walked by this tree, it energetically nudged me to meditate with it.

I've heard that people do it, the most famous of all being Buddha. However, I didn't actually know how to meditate and harmonize my energy with that of that tree; it had been so long since I had actually felt close to nature because of, you know, the whole getting lost in the system and trying to be 'normal.' Still, I sat down and attempted to meditate with the tree. It took me about 20 minutes to get a really good connection with it. But once I started meditating with it, I felt myself kind of drift off into this visualization which I believe the tree was giving me. And I was like, "Well, what's happening here?" I started to pay attention to the visuals. Realizing what was happening, I was like, "Oh my gosh, the tree is trying to communicate with me!" I was really excited but tried to calm myself down and concentrate.

I decided to surrender to what the tree was trying to tell me. And what the tree showed me was two Native Americans, like a father and a son, going through the woods. The father was teaching his son how to hunt, gather, and whatnot. It was like a really soulful, loving connection between them. I watched them catch some game and fish, and then they took it back to the family. It was an essence of primal beauty – back when man had a deeper connection with nature. Then, all of a sudden, it showed me a farmer and his son, from what seemed like within the last 100 years, on a tractor just kind of harvesting the field, trading some of the produce, and bringing in food back home to the family. They had a nice dinner table in front of a big bay window with light coming through, and the family members seated at the table were all soulfully enjoying each other's company and really celebrating the small things in life. Seeing all this, I was like, "Oh, this is very beautiful, but why are you showing me a father and a child? I was listening to the tree intently for an answer, and then, all of a sudden, I saw that the Native American father and his son, now older.

The tree was showing me a faceoff between two tribes, one led by the father and the other by his son, now their respective chiefs. Somehow, over the years, they got angry with each other, and now they were against each other, ready for violence. As the two tribes faced off against one another, I felt not just anger and also a lot of egos. The tree was telling me what harm ego does, and I was kind of sad for this relationship because just prior, it had been so beautiful – the connections they were making and the bond they had some 20 years earlier.

The tree made sure that I knew that ego was what came between them. Then after, it switched me to a frame where it showed the farmer in a hospital bed alone with like an IV in his arm, dying of cancer. Meanwhile, his son sitting at home looking out the window, really sad and angry, but it appears that he was shut off from his father as if something happened between them that caused his son to refuse to see him. The tree showed me this as another way that ego presented itself. Seeing all this, I was just like, "Oh man, this is sad…" Then I asked, "Okay, is there anything more you know?" The tree went a little deeper, showing me visuals and showed roots growing down and connecting to my diaphragm.

And it said, "Where in you are you presenting with ego towards those you've had soulful connections to in the past?" I was just like blown away by that question because I didn't even understand it. At the time, I really didn't know what ego was fully; I would be just like, "Okay, I just know ego gets in the way of the eternal being within us that wants to lead."

Then my parents came up, and I then realized how I had been shut down by my parents due to anger and vice versa. I realized that this tree was trying to help me understand and bring awareness to things within me so that it could heal me it. I was just so thankful for the tree, and when I opened my eyes, still in a trance-like state, the tree showed me a silhouette of a father holding his son's hand, symbolizing the times when we were appreciative and actually connected with each other fully. As I came back to my physical reality, I saw that the tree looked like it had been two trees intertwined together, as if the tree had served a past life as a human.

It took me a while to digest, understand, and integrate into my mind this phenomenally otherworldly experience. From there on, I started meditating with trees all the time, and the trees would tell me stories and fables of the past that resonated with me, my life, and my connections.

Through them, they would give me lessons about what humanity needed to overcome. I spent the whole spring and summer meditating with the trees, and it inspired me to start looking into Kundalini yoga. I started just kind of researching other ways that I could get deeper into my intuition and start figuring out myself so that I can help others figure out themselves when it comes to repairing the things, we don't know how to repair within ourselves that are more emotionally and energetically based rather than physically.

At this stage of my journey, I was finally seeing myself as more than an acupuncturist. I was seeing that I was here to help others with much more than just their mind and body connectivity; I was here to help with their Mind-Body-Soul alignment, energy activation, and transformation. I knew that the next stage of my journey had now begun.

CHAPTER 9
SPIRITUAL AWAKENING

It was a normal day, and everything seemed to be going as planned. I was working as usual, and suddenly, I felt the shift in the air. There was something different about this day. We all knew a flu virus was happening in the U.S, but we didn't know that it would soon be turned into a contagious and dangerous incurable virus by the name of Covid-19. I started receiving notifications at the same hour from many different companies and vendors that my practice is affiliated with. My inbox was consistently buzzing, and every email had a subject line that reassured their products or services were being protected and properly handled to prevent the spread of covid-19.

I looked up at my receptionist with a blank face, and we both knew something strange was happening. I could feel so much fear, more than I had ever felt at once, with a knowing that it wasn't mine. Then, what happened next, confirmed the energy that I was feeling. The W.H.O announced that Covid-19 is a pandemic and people must leave work unless it was considered essential & stay indoors. This had never happened before so I had so many questions as to why there was so much ambiguity and confusion and fear behind these new mandates. For how long? It wasn't told back then. All the businesses were shutting down, work-from-home was implemented, the grocery stores rushed up, and chaos was in the air.

People were reacting in fear, and I just thought about it as another viral infection, but eventually after a few days of being isolated, I started to feel the fear in myself as well. I was afraid but didn't let it affect me too much initially. I just had a newborn baby who was three months old at that time. I was living with my child's father. I felt a lot of love towards him and had hoped to create a bigger family with him in time. I had never had this much time to myself as My child's grandmother loved to take him from me for a few hours daily so I could keep up with my self-care and continue to seek guidance for the next steps to take since my business was my only source of income to help pay for the bills.

Businesses were completely shut down. The grocery stores had limited hours, and the entire U.S was under lockdown. Every day, the government announced new policies. I felt a thick cloud of fear, guilt and shame accumulating over time over everyone. People were agitated with the new government policies; everybody wanted to know more about what was happening, panic and chaos were on the peek, and nobody behaved as they once did. I started to feel different about myself when I observed people panicking so much. I had negative thoughts, but I was still happy to be home and spend time with my baby & what I had hoped to be able to bond as a family. I wanted to figure out a way I could work online to earn money while I waited for the return to my normal life.

I stayed at home with my son, and watched in horror as huge emergencies and crises after crisis were reported in the media. No physical contact among people. The hyped-up talk of this contagious disease and the numerous reports of large quantities of deaths due to it, made me feel uneasy about going outside in public. People stopped communicating, and I felt negative & stagnant energy in myself. I felt disconnected from the outside world and even from parts of myself so I stopped watching the news and decided to use this extra time to continue my education and to invest in myself.

Since I had delivered my baby, I hadn't had time to reflect or reevaluate what direction I wanted to continue moving my services in. I was feeling better in my own energy field at home and started searching online for ways I could use my skills online. I wanted to use this time to be productive and earn some money that could help me settle on my entrepreneurship career. I didn't know how we were going to pay my bills, how we would manage all of the payments for my practice, and how we would afford other expenses. I just thought, "I would be okay." At the same, without realizing this fully as I was starting to discover a part of myself, I had never been able to fully explore consciously, my child's father thought something different.

I came across esoteric benefits of meditating, and it caught my mind during my research on passive income. But I didn't pursue it right away until one day, I was sitting on my couch, and the sun was shining through the curtains inside onto the back of my neck. I was in the middle of taking a selfie as I had this overwhelming urge to document the blissful energy shift, I was consciously experiencing at that moment. When I clicked the picture, all I could see was the beautiful shining sunlight and the colored rainbows in the background of my picture. The air felt good, and the sun's warmth made me realize that it was the sun that was helping to facilitate the blissful energy shift I was experiencing at that moment. My entire self-changed, and all I wanted to do was meditate.

Now that I think back to that day, I discovered that I was having a spiritual awakening. I went beyond my boundaries and took my first step toward evolution. I experienced my divinity which was representing a paradigm shift of the highest order. This spiritual awakening had the potential to rip apart reality and take me to a new life of conscious growth and evolution. One that I felt I had been waiting for my entire life to show up. It felt as if I was emerging from a deep sleep; I was able to see the dream for what it truly was – an illusion from which there can be no going back. I started doing meditation more often. where meditation might have been difficult to do in the past, I could do it whenever, wherever. It made me feel better, and I thought I was becoming a better self of myself, what you could say, an upgraded version.

I decided that I wanted to meditate professionally, as I was seeing a change in my inner self. I started feeling better about my surroundings, the fear vanished, and all I knew was that everything would be okay and that humanity was being initiated to start healing. I worked on Yoga programs and attended a lot of online healing workshops during this timeframe. I had this idea of learning how to teach meditation online so that I could still help others in their healing process at home and still be able to bring in some extra income. I was hoping to add this as another service at the practice to give the patient more skills to connect back to themselves and nurture their life force with.

I learned all about how to start teaching it, how it benefits you, and why you should do it. I then started helping people around me. I posted about it on my social media platforms. I told them about how meditation could help restructure their nervous system. I answered a lot of queries from people asking me about meditation. I saw potential in this area and hired an online coach to help me work professionally and set up an online presence with this. This was when everything changed for me.

My partner at the time was upset with me for investing money in myself and for putting the online coach on my personal credit card. I guess he didn't see this as a good idea or helpful to my potential. He expressed that he saw it as a waste of my money. I was living in his house, but I was an independent and working woman for a long time. He made me feel as if I wasn't allowed to invest in myself or try to reach my full potential through healing and self-discovery. Even with my intentions being to help bring more forms of income into the family. He was upset that I had made this decision without him so he asked me to leave his house. He was hurtful to me and even tried to spin my own spiritual awakening against me as an emotional episode of instability. I was not sure what to do as I was embarking on something that was bigger than myself so I started asking for help and guidance from the universe as I meditated.

& Then one day shortly after, while feeling somewhat helpless to my situation, I was visited by Goddess Kali Ma. She showed up in my mind's eye with loving and nurturing energy. Telepathically she told me that she was with me to protect me and to help me see the truth about what was really happening with humanity and what we are lost in. She told me not to worry and that she would be there right behind me with all of her arms to help ward off anyone who is sick with their ego, who may try to harm me. I wasn't sure if this was real as it was my first encounter with a known god before. I didn't know much about the Hindu belief system but I know I had always been drawn to it. I felt her energy around me for a few days as she would continue to help me feel her presence through meditation, through my research and through divination tools. I accepted her as one of my protectors as she lifted the veil from my eyes. & To my surprise I saw why my partner at the time was behaving the way that he was. I wasn't in agreement with it but I could see the programs and the wounds behind the words much more clearly. The male domination, the misogynistic way of ruling through fear and repression. The deception, the manipulations, the tactics. Everything started to reveal itself to me and although it was not very pretty, I was grateful to finally make sense of the misalignment that I had always felt in this world.

I didn't let my partner's words interfere with my newfound knowledge although his words did hurt me deeply at times considering I was in love with him and had a child with him who was now getting caught up in this psychological warfare that I didn't intentionally ask for.

Goddess Kali was with me through the entire crumbling of my foundation, she would let me know in advance when I would receive an attack from the male ego by showing me a spider three times in a row within an hour. She would then help me mentally prepare and call her prior to the attack so I would feel protected and strong enough to stand up for myself if I was called to do so..

I was not very good at this initially as my ego would be triggered too but over time, I was able to get to the point where I would be able to plant seeds with whomever was attacking me to reflect back on eventually and realize that I was mostly always just trying to explain my viewpoint from a higher consciousness perspective and or restore balance and peace to the equation. The problem with this was that it was mistaken and misunderstood as me trying to "act smarter than them" and also trying to "deflect", which would just fuel and irritate the ego more.

I kept moving forward, it was all that I could do, and I started searching for new places around my existing area. I found a place in the country on a quiet side road, so I shifted there. Though I was heartbroken because nothing had played out as I had originally planned. Thus, this was the first illusion that completely shattered and shifted my life, as I continued to move through the layers of deception I had found myself lost in, which I continued to keep track of because in turn I knew I would eventually try to figure out a way to help others through experiences similar to mine.

I used my time alone to focus on meditation, and I also started to discover interesting correlations with astrology. I read more about it in-depth and was shocked to know what it was showing me. The American Revolution, the shifts in mankind, and changes happening all around the world. I was more interested in playing in this field & linking it to the patterns I was seeing and feeling and learning in myself, in humanity & in the natural world. I also started practicing oracle and tarot cards. I facetimed my friends and colleagues and did oracle and tarot reading for them. just to practice and to receive feedback.

Even though I had just started, what stunned me the most about this experience was that everything I read in the oracle and tarot cards would resonate with the person I was speaking to. I noticed that I could feel into their energy field somehow even being on the other end of a screen. I was able to describe what I was feeling to them and many of them would stare blankly almost in tears sometimes as I did their readings. I sometimes felt as if it wasn't me who was reading those cards. But someone else.

I dug deeper and started working with the moon, the full moon, and the new moon. I was able to heal layers and release energies that were no longer serving my highest good. I was able to manifest money by doing this, and it helped me with the bills. It helped me to expand into a more authentic version of myself, to help me gain confidence and recover from insecurities that were blocking me from being able to achieve my highest potential.

All throughout my house I would play healing frequencies and sound baths as I would make note of how the experience of listening to sound was helping me heal as I felt the shifts within my body and as I paid attention to the memories and to the emotions that were showing up for me to re-evaluate and understand differently. I was passionately devoted to the healing and learning how to heal process during this time. I no longer allowed myself to pay attention to who was judging me or constantly wanting to guilt and shame me for being selfish, for not being the person who others felt I was supposed to be to them. Instead, I was moving ahead during the time of the Pandemic and doing everything in my power to prepare myself for a mission where I would need to be operating from a more expansive and hybrid approach of helping others heal. Because I knew more was coming, and that this was going to be the beginning of a lot of change, the most change anyone has ever experienced or lived through in centuries. I knew in my soul that I was preparing for something really big, natural laws and forces were confirming it as it was all I trusted at that time. Even though he was angry and it was painful to acknowledge at the time, I also knew that my ex-partner would eventually understand what I was doing in the times to come.

After returning to work I noticed how paralyzed my patients were from the fear and from the covid shutdown. People all around me were fighting, arguing, acting aggressive, being judgmental and obsessively worried about unemployment and bills, it was more chaotic than I had expected it to be. I had started to understand my natural pace better at that point and I was trying to figure out how to work this into my work schedule. The chaos of the outer world felt extremely different from my world at home. Because on my own time I was nurturing my life force and cleansing my energy field and meditating. Traveling into the depths of my inner being and doing soul retrievals from past times lines to reclaim my power to help me move forward and to help restore balance for the greater good of all. I felt like I was becoming my own superhero and I knew that I was going to eventually find a way to help others out of their suffering through these self-discoveries as well.

I knew that if I figured out how to heal and shift my inner world into what I was shown in my meditations, it would eventually start to reflect outwardly. And that is exactly what happened, I saw major shifts happen around me as I would work through my kundalini yoga program. It was like the universe would kick anyone out of my life suddenly, unexpectedly and sometimes chaotically if they were interfering with my mission and dreams. It was like the universe was keeping an eye on those who were closest to me so that I could continue on with my journey and not be drawn away or distracted from my mission through sabotage, envy and ulterior motives. I realized that I was no longer operating solely from the physical world; I was recovering my inherent multidimensional nature. This was the beginning of my journey to being able to channel higher dimensional beings. Goddess Kali came in to initiate my awakening so that I would be able to help aid as a bridge in the healing, the transformation and the evolution of mankind.

CHAPTER 10
THE DARK NIGHT OF THE SOUL

After receiving my mission everything changed.

I had to heal and shed my way to the future version of myself that I was fortunate enough to receive glimpses of in my meditations. She was meditating in a Forest clearing where light poured onto and around her. She had animals walking towards her as she was receiving the light through her crown chakra. She was wearing crystal jewelry and she was extremely comfortable & grounded in her body. She was tan and toned like she did yoga and core work regularly. She had a peacefulness to her and a self-acceptance about her that made me feel as if she was my highest timeline.

She had a glow, a vitality about her. She was pure and she radiated love. When I saw her, I knew I had to become her. She felt like the best possible version of me.

What I didn't realize when I accepted this vision as my future self was that I was going to have to face all of my wounds and all of my karma to get to her. The lessons mostly played out in interpersonal relationships. Anyone I would get close to would eventually reject me because of how much I triggered their shadow. It was hard having light that attracted easily and dark that repelled them over time consistently. I would also be easily triggered by any behavior that felt repressive or controlling. It was like I was going back into my childhood again but this time as an adult with more knowledge and better coping mechanisms.

I did my best working through the shadow as time allowed. I grew impatient with myself and then realized that I needed to work on my own self-worth as well but ultimately as I continued to follow the clues and nudges from my soul, I was able to unlock and see behind the wounds that would reveal themselves to me and I started discerning what was authentically mine vs what was conditioned, learned or programmed into my mind.

I also realized that this work takes patience, understanding and compassion to move through with myself and with others around me as I was evolving and shifting through timelines rapidly.

I couldn't see it then but looking back now, I can imagine how fast paced & chaotic all of this would have seemed to someone who wasn't able to see or feel what I was experiencing. Although I did receive a lot of criticism and some backlash for transparently speaking my truth to everyone I was close with and through social media to my community, eventually they either distanced themselves or grew to accept me for my new authentic and open way of being. Some even started to embrace some of the methods I was discovering towards the healing process along the way.

Over time my methods would lead to many creative ideas, a few more businesses to aid in passive forms of income for mine and my child's foundation and also more ways of helping others connect fully back to their life force and begin the healing journey that Goddess Kali Ma initiated and showed within me. Hence, I was becoming an activator of soul.

I was also noticing that I was helping my patients step into leadership positions with their jobs and their careers by helping them reclaim their power. I was seeing beautiful transformations happen all around me by utilizing my new services and through sharing what I was seeing and articulating from what was being shown to me in my meditations and how it paired with the astrology that I was researching daily. I started to see my spiritual awakening and transformation process inspire, trigger and or activate everyone around me.

During one of my meditations, I was asked to visit Sedona AZ, a well-known healing vortex in the states. I was asked to go there to heal and to activate my light body. It was my first travel assignment with the universe. I went there with no plan. My soul led the way. It led me to healers who would help me understand my level of consciousness, a UFO tour where we looked into the night sky with night vision goggles to see a lot of traffic in the sky that can't be seen with the naked eye & a paranormal experience.

The sojourn led me to the red rocks where I meditated and in this meditation I saw Joan of arc stand up to a council and offer to help me on my mission. An hour after seeing Joan, I went with my travel partner who was recording footage of the trip to a Korean BBQ place for lunch. In the Korean BBQ place, I saw a group of rainbows spinning orbs later I found out they were merkabahs come into the restaurant and circle around me. My friend couldn't see the orbs but he could feel the heat of them and also the light from them reflected off of my earrings into the camera. He told me that his hands were on fire as he was holding the camera up and recording. This experience felt extremely confusing as I was trying to remain calm with it being in public but I was also nervous not being able to explain the paranormal phenomena I was experiencing in the physical without anyone else being able to actually see it too.

I felt as if the orbs were downloading information into my head. I started to experience a headache after a few minutes. The whole experience lasted about 8 minutes. And then they were gone and everything was calm. We ate our lunch and then went to the car to watch the footage. You couldn't see the orbs but the video was delayed and distorted and it had a weird noise in the background of it. We went to the red rocks to meditate and my headache disappeared almost immediately. I went to re watch the footage later that night and the video looked normal and the noise was no longer in the background. All of this was confirming that whatever I was doing was definitely showing up in my physical reality. That night as I was sleeping an angel visited me in my dreams and told me that I was going to wake up in a month with a new gift. That everything I had experienced the day prior would take a month to integrate into my body and allow me to utilize my new gift. A month later I was miraculously able to do quantum healing. I was given this gift to help heal the inner child through the quantum realm. I was given this gift to help others gain access to the quantum realm and learn to timeline hop. All of this was new to me so it took me about a year to really understand the details of what I was doing and how I was doing it but it was working and I was receiving a lot of positive feedback from clients who did the inner child healing exercises with me and overcame wounds and fears they had no idea how to see past or even access. To me this was revolutionary, as I felt hopeless to the idea of healing after experiencing so many modalities throughout my life that couldn't reach the depth of what I needed. It was like I had discovered and somehow found a way to structure a new way of healing and unifying the self.

More channels came in on how to operate from mind body soul perspective and also on how to differentiate egoic program from soul expression. Channels on how to process an emotion also showed up and that as humans we should be spending at least 3-5 hours a week reflecting and processing emotions that we didn't have time to work through fully throughout the week while we are also working through our daily and weekly responsibilities and obligations.

The more I was able to lead with soul the more authentic and natural I started to feel and become.

All of this was a miracle to me, as I had not fully understood the disconnect between myself and this reality until I realized I was meant to be a bridge for it. The trip to Sedona AZ vortex led me to more vortexes after with themes of what I would be experiencing at them. Soulfully I followed these nudges and my whole world around me continued to change and transform as I stayed committed to the mission and as I continued to learn the details of how I would continue to carry it out while I was moving closer and closer to my highest self.

CHAPTER 11
THE QUANTUM FIELD

As I was working through trying to manage a high contact profession during a pandemic and also trying to figure out how to get to my higher self who would appear to me whenever I would look for her in my meditations. I felt as if I was living in an entirely different world than those around me and it was like I was crawling to work to make sure the bills were getting paid and that patients were finding peace in a time of dark despair. I was doing everything in my power to make sense of all of these new timelines I was able to access. So, while working with the moon I was able to start really feeling into and getting a better handle on identifying and protecting myself from the different energies that were coming at me and causing delays in my progress. I'll admit that it felt like I was living in multiple dimensions at once but I was still trying my hardest to continue doing the inner work to help make positive shifts in my physical reality. I would receive visions of the Ancient Egyptian gods around this point and I was taking care of a family of blue jays that came in around the same time as the blue avians started visiting me and sending me information in my dream state. I could tell that anyone who tried spending time with me at that point would get frustrated or annoyed with me if I tried talking about everything that I was experiencing, so I had to limit what I said in front of those who weren't able to understand what I was saying or even experiencing. Which was almost everyone. It was almost like anytime I would bring up what I was experiencing everyone around me would try to silence me or be embarrassed about what I was speaking of so they would eventually reject and/or leave my energy field over time as they started to feel disconnected from me. As I started to spend more time alone in my own energy field, I started receiving premonitions and messages from the universe at random times of the day during the week sometimes while I was driving, while I was treating and while I was sitting in silence. These premonitions were coming in to mentally prepare me for the upcoming events that would take place.

Around this timeframe Mary Magdalene also started watching over me as I slept. She watched over me like she was mothering me. One day while I was starting my vehicle to take My son to daycare, I heard a song begin perfectly as the vehicle started. "Maybe it's time to let the old ways die, maybe it's time to let the old ways die." It just seemed too perfect for the song to start at the same time as I had turned the key to start the vehicle. As I was thinking this and singing along while driving, I had missed my turn and had to turn around in a church parking lot and as I was turning around, I received a massive download of information. The sensation of a download feels like an adrenaline rush. All of the chakras activate I feel my crown chakra tingle and bring in information and then bam it's just up to me to start automatically writing or speaking it. I started recording these occurrences because they always happened so randomly. This particular download spoke of humanity needing to start clearing the cycles of suffering in their pain body (emotional stagnant energy) or else the body would self-destruct with the new upgrades coming in for the body in the years to come.

The download explained how a series of events would continue to happen that would turn science upside down and make everyone question reality as we know it. I was expected to put this information out there somehow and in some way. I hadn't tapped into my creative potential yet so I was still working on esoteric mind body soul alignment protocols and recording & writing the channels that I was continuously receiving out on the side. I started sitting with the information and doing research to make sure this information was actually valid information. To my surprise I was seeing a prelude in this physical reality to what these premonitions coming in were pertaining to and I started to create systems and protocols to help release the pain body.

I was able to work with the new quantum healing techniques that I had been gifted through the inner child activation meditation that I had created which is meant to unify the past present and future and shows the client how to work in the quantum realm alongside their inner child and higher self in order to shift their life into their highest timeline.

And then while helping clients reunite with their inner child, I discovered how to help them process emotions trapped in their body by helping them understand how the human operates from a mind body soul perspective . I was able to break this down simply so they could easily observe, clear and emotionally process their wounds, ego blocks, limiting beliefs and programs that do not fall into alignment with who they currently are or who they are trying to shift into. This helped them heal and shift as I had given them a tool to work through the pain body and release what was considered blockage to them that was stuck in their energy field.

This was a success as my clients started handling conflict better as they started to heal and see themselves in a better light. This also in turn strengthened their vitality, allowed them to focus on learning other healthy coping mechanisms for returning to their center and as they were feeling better emotionally it improved their overall physical health. They were advocating for themselves and breaking unhealthy cycles in their lives and feeling more connected to themselves and to those who were in alignment with who they were and trying to become. Just the simple protocol to stop and actually move through a few questions when the body lets the mind know that it's carrying too much information to function the way it's designed to function.

Also operating from a mind body soul perspective is vital to gaining access to your gifts and also to your highest timelines. It's all about increasing self-awareness and being patient with yourself by remembering that the mind is like a mother board of input and output of stimulation, it is not meant to process the emotions alone. You need to be fully connected to your soul and your body to help the mind process the emotions, so at first it is important to set time apart each week 3-5 hours starting out to meditate and allow the body to show you what it needs you to go through that has not been fully processed. This self-care act allows one to thoroughly go through a memory or an emotion rises up and look at it from all different perspectives in order to fully appreciate and or properly respond to an experience that they have had that they weren't sure how they truly felt or needed to respond with intuitively.

This enforces and encourages one to build a mind body soul connection and it strengthens a person's intuition. It also helps them gain emotional intelligence by being able to see a situation with emotion attached from multiple angles. So, remembering that when the mind experiences something from physical reality, if emotion is attached to it, it will store it in the body for you to work through later so the mind can carry out its daily interactions in the physical. If triggered from a backup of unprocessed emotions, the ego will switch on and turn your fight or flight response on inside the body to alert you to find you safety or to refrain from anymore experiences that you are unsure of how to respond to. When a backup of emotions show up as a reactive trigger it's usually rooted deeply in a fear or a wound and that is something that is vital to take time out to process and unpack as it will only cause harm to the mind and the body the longer it builds and stays unprocessed in the human and the humans energy field. Over time if we aren't clearing the unprocessed information from our emotional and physical body, it will start to create barriers around the heart space which will block your soul from being able to access your body fully. The heart is considered the house or the seat of the soul. Now all of this information was given to me through visuals and channels so it's simplified to help others understand how to do it without the in-depth knowledge to truly understand the physiological workings of it. It is meant to help humanity heal and release the pain body effectively to understand the importance of emotional and intuitive intelligence when operating in this physical reality to avoid early self-destruction of the mind and the body and when practice often will continuously activate and nurture your relationship to the eternal life force of the soul within you.

CHAPTER 12
CONCLUSION

And so it came to pass that as I continued to uncover more information pertaining to my inner universe, I unraveled and revealed many other interesting aspects about myself and also much information to help aid in developing more harmonious systems to operate in for highest possible potential for the future of mankind. Through my research and healing process, I eventually discovered that my spiritual awakening happened during the height of a 6-and-a-half-year karmic cycle which is otherwise known as "Saturn return" which I hadn't even realized I was in until the last 3 months of it. After I had realized I was working through a karmic cycle everything made even more sense as spiritual awakenings can commonly happen during these difficult periods in one's life.

So, in hindsight, all of what I had experienced during the last few years that was negative, traumatic and harmful ended up serving as a catalyst to dive deeper into the depths of my inner being. To finally remember my calling. To reunite with my natural frequency of my inner child and to reach my highest timeline through my future self.

By doing this, I have been able to find parallels between the light and the dark and I have been able to learn how to alchemize and transmute the energies that I carry within to help change and shift the energies showing up for me in my outer physical reality.

Through this experience I have humbly accepted myself as continuing to serve as a bridge between many levels of consciousness and I have given myself permission to continue learning and navigating these abilities and skills to help aid in the continuation of alleviating the unnecessary sufferings of humanity, and helping to liberate them from where they have psychologically found themselves enslaved.

The main theme that is continuously sent through to me from the blue avians, from the Sun and from Earth is that humanity needs to heal and that we also need to integrate back with the Earth so that we may be able to heal more effectively, so we are able to receive the upgrades from our solar system so that we may allow ourselves to shift back into multidimensional beings, and so that we may restore our life force and receive further instruction on how to move forward from our internal navigation systems.

This whole experience reminds me of and can be compared to "the hero's journey" almost as perfectly as it was written in a metaphorical way. If there is anything I ask of you to take with you from my story, as I have been asked to write many more with the information that has shown up and is continuously pouring through me. For this particular story, I ask that you take the time to learn to love yourself and that you take the time to get to know yourself fully, as you are your own unique and amazing universe full of many gifts and wonders to learn from and to experience.

I also ask that we remain conscious of the fact that the children will always come in with a higher consciousness and with open access to their gifts as it is divinely designed this way to help aid in the progression and evolution of mankind, to be able to fit into the era where they will stay with or wake up fully to themselves in and be able to play out their unique part in this human experience for the evolution of their own human and for the evolution of mankind. This will also serve well to the evolution of their soul which is identified as an eternal life force which ultimately aids in the evolution of the universe and of the true creator of existence.

I also ask that you think about how our current systems have shown where they are not helpful or overly corrupt to the point of where it has been interfering with this divine process. Commit to creating more stable foundations for new systems that are designed to help us move forward on our trajectory. Integrate new technology and also our systems of navigation and operation as a human with the natural laws of the universe and with the natural biorhythms of Earth, so that we may stay in harmony with all systems of influence and so that we may honor her and represent her properly and most appropriately in the times to come and further out into the future when we go into the galactic era.

With all of this being said this is the end of my story, it is a quick overview of my human life so far and it is meant to serve as an example of how those who have experienced similar hardships and abuse as I have, can look back and possibly see themselves in my story, as a child born into a reality that you were forced to conform to with confusion all around you not knowing how to function or fit in, but knowing that you had to figure it out for the survival of your own soul. To find or receive guides to help you along the way, and to one day wake back up to yourself to finally heal from it all. So that you may continue to learn how to carry out and work towards completing your mission.

My parting way to this whole experience that we have just went on together will be a question; and that question is;

Do you remember what your mission is?

Made in the USA
Coppell, TX
23 March 2023

14671701R00059